Titian

Electa / Art Books International

Self Portrait, c. 1562. Berlin, Staatliche Museen.

Titian

No artist was ever more a painter than Titian. Perhaps only Velasquez and Van Gogh equalled him in their feeling for colour. Titian's every brush stroke meant not just a new colour laid on the canvas but form, mass and substance. One of his sayings was that to be a painter one only need know three colours: white, red and black, "and be able to use them." This concept of painting, developed in the mid-sixteenth century, was embodied in an output remarkable both in its quality and its quantity, and wholly antithetical to the "primacy of drawing" asserted in the same period by Michelangelo. Titian and Michelangelo were the two pillars of art in the sixteenth century. Their work created a new concept of art and the role of the artist in society. Michelangelo was the classical example of the solitary, desperate, creative mind, living in anguish. Titian was a successful practitioner of his art, a professional who achieved all his objectives and accumulated great wealth. Titian's life can be interpreted in two ways. On the one hand he was a painter of extraordinary energy, who revolutionized technique and influenced every generation of artists, virtually down to our own times. On the other he had a shrewd business sense of a surprisingly modern kind; he organized his professional life on a financial basis, not without a touch of cynicism towards his competitors.

In both these ways Titian was an entirely new kind of figure, with no predecessors and with very few successors. He handled colour with intense passion, passing from the limpid, harmonious tones of his early work to the increasingly thick, heavy impasto of his later years, with the paint laid on with richly dramatic brushstrokes; yet at the same time he ran his workshop and administered his investments with a solid practical sense. Dividing his attention between the burning excitement of the colours on his canvases and a stubborn insistence on getting a good price for his work, Titian raised the status of the artist from that of a tradesman to a skilled professional. To do so he reorganized his workshop, making unprecedented use of a network of publicity: this led to his partnership with Pietro Aretino, who in practice acted as his sales agent, finding clients abroad, especially in Spain. Titian artfully created his own myth: for sixty years he was the official painter to the Venetian Republic, an authentic patriarch of Venetian art. Titian was alive and still active when the first accounts of his life and art were being published, so that we can follow events almost day by day. The master's art and biography became the stuff of legend; Titian was credited with almost divine qualities. Yet, as his letters and above all his paintings show, this boy who had descended from the mountains of Cadore to renew the history of art, never lost contact with the realities of daily life, with the bitter-sweet taste of the life which pulsates so vividly in his masterpieces.

Early Enthusiasms and Rise to Supremacy in Venetian Art (1490–1518)

We know virtually everything of Titian's life, except for his date of birth, which can be conjecturally placed between 1488 and 1490 at Pieve di Cadore. Pieve di Cadore was an important town in the Dolomites, with a thriving timber industry. Titian later invested large sums in saw-mills and shipments of timber for the Arsenal in Venice. The Vecellio family was well-known and respected in the town, with generations of lawyers, scriveners and public officials among its members. Titian, the second child of Gregorio Vecellio, no doubt absorbed this professional mentality, and even as a boy he applied it in an original fashion to his painter's workshop. Endowed with a marked natural talent, Titian left Pieve di Cadore when he was nine years old, together with his brother Francesco (his future collaborator). In the first decade of the sixteenth century, a period of far-reaching changes in Venetian art, Titian completed the stages of his apprenticeship, firstly under the mosaicist Sebastiano Zuccato, then under Gentile Bellini and finally with Giovanni Bellini. From his first master the adolescent Titian learnt to handle colour as matter: Zuccato's workshop was employed on the interminable task of the decoration of the church of San Marco. Titian would have been able to touch the coloured mosaic tiles, feel their weight and texture. Then under Gentile Bellini he learnt the skills of portraiture, as well as the ability to organize large compositions. Gentile was skilled at painting huge narrative works, like the immense *Saint Mark Preaching in Alexandria*, now in the Pinacoteca di Brera in Milan.

Then coming under Giovanni, Titian completed his training by acquiring his most important skill: "tonal" painting. This was the great achievement of Venetian painting on the threshold of the Cinquecento, the outstanding accomplishment of Giovanni Bellini and soon after developed further by Giorgione and Titian himself. Essentially the Venetian Renaissance painters wanted to obtain the effects of natural light falling on landscape and figures, so they gradually abandoned the use of draw-

ing and instead laid their colours on directly, with subtle gradations of tone between light and shade.
The synthesis of these experiments appears in the first important work painted by the youthful Titian: the *Saint Peter Altarpiece* (Royal Museum of Fine Arts, Antwerp), commissioned by Jacopo Pesaro. This painting also shows the first signs of his relationship with Giorgione, which turned into full collaboration in 1508. Titian worked with the young but already successful painter on the immense task of decorating the façades of the Fondaco dei Tedeschi, a huge warehouse by the Rialto, rebuilt after being seriously damaged by fire. Giorgione was in charge of the work and executed the main façade facing the Grand Canal, leaving Titian the side facing the Mercerie. The few surviving fragments, preserved in the Galleria Franchetti at the Ca' d'Oro, suggest the profound differences between the two artists: the *Nude* by Giorgione has a tranquil softness within the shadowy niche for which it was painted, while Titian's image of *Justice* is a dynamic figure, in full and sweeping movement, unhampered by any architectural elements. Titian absorbed the poetic world of Giorgione, making contact with the same clients, and adapted his style to Giorgione's to a degree that astonished his contemporaries; yet even so he was already endowed with a temperament all his own, beginning to win a public and a name.
Between 1508 and 1510 his partnership with Giorgione produced works like the *Concert* now in the Louvre, the *Christ Carrying the Cross* in the Scuola Grande di San Rocco in Venice, and the Dresden *Venus*. Titian also mastered Giorgione's technique as a portraitist, with half-length figures, half-turned to the viewer, painted with minute, patient brush-strokes, careful to render the delicacy of every detail of the sitter's features and clothing.
The plague epidemic that caused Giorgione's death late in 1510 gave Titian the chance to become the leading figure in the Venetian art world. Giovanni Bellini, the official painter to the Venetian Republic, was now well over eighty, Vittore Carpaccio's talents had begun to decline, and Lorenzo Lotto had left the Veneto for the Marches and Rome. His only rival might have been another artist from the circle of Giorgione, Sebastiano Luciani (better known by his later nickname, Sebastiano "del Piombo"), but Titian possessed the energy and forcefulness needed to clear the field of all adversaries. In Padua, in April 1511, he frescoed three *Miracles of Saint Anthony* in the Scuola di Sant'Antonio (Plate 1): their bold compositional energy and the use of Giorgionesque colour for scenes that were no longer subtly melancholy but richly dramatic convinced Sebastiano that he had an insuperable adversary in his former companion of study under Giorgione.
Soon after, having returned to Venice after the plague had ended, Titian painted the votive altarpiece of *Saint Mark Enthroned* (now in the sacristy of Santa Maria della Salute; Plate 2), and his fame was by this time considerable. These works with their elegant composition and refined grasp of natural details were the basis of the youthful master's solid commercial success. By 1513 Titian owned a thriving workshop of his own, and in that year he received his first official commission, an impressive historical painting for the Doge's Palace. But he worked above all for private clients, Venetian patricians and

Madonna with Saints, detail with self portrait as a young man. Madrid, Museo del Prado.

Engraving of the lost altarpiece of San Zanipolo.

merchants from the north of Europe, alternating religious and profane subjects: the *Noli Me Tangere* in the National Gallery, London (Plate 3), the *Three Ages of Man* in Edinburgh, the *Sacra Conversazione* in the Fondazione Magnani Rocca at Mamiano, the *Sacred and Profane Love* in the Galleria Borghese, Rome (Plate 4). In this last great work, Titian triumphally asserted the warm, vibrant use of tonalism, with richly sensuous results. These years also produced numerous portraits (*The Ailing Man* in the Uffizi, the *Girl in a Fur Coat* in the Frick Collection of New York) and half-length female figures (the *Flora* in the Uffizi, the *Violante* in Vienna, the *Girl with a Mirror* in the Louvre), which helped to consolidate his reputation and wealth. By this time Titian had become the most important artist in Venice. 1516 was a crucial year in the history of Venice and Titian's career. The treaty of Noyon restored all the territories Venice had lost eight years earlier in the war of the League of Cambray, and a period of new optimism began. Against this background it is clear that the painting of the *Assunta* (Plate 5), for the high altar of the church of the Frari possessed a richly symbolic role. Titian received the commission for this work in 1516. In November of the same year Giovanni Bellini died, and Titian was appointed in his place official painter to the Venetian Republic, a post he held till his death.

The *Assunta*, completed and exhibited publicly in 1518, set the seal on his youthful work. The immense size of this altarpiece led Titian to adopt a new structure for the composition, with figures of unusual dimensions sustained by the exceptional intensity of the colouring. The painting aroused great bewilderment when it was first unveiled because of its unconventional treatment of the subject, but the astonishment was soon transformed into delight.

International Fame and the Masterpieces of Titian's Early Maturity (1518–1538)

Alfonso d'Este, the Duke of Ferrara, was the first nobleman outside Venice to commission important works from Titian, frequently inviting him to reside in his court. Between 1518 and 1521 Titian was engaged on the decoration of the duke's private study, unfortunately dismantled in 1595. He also retouched Giovanni Bellini's *Feast of the Gods*, radically altering the landscape, and executed the three Bacchanals (the *Andrians*, Plate 7, and the *Worship of Venus* are in the Prado, *Bacchus and Ariadne*, Plate 8, is in the National Gallery, London). These painting are filled with joyful festivity, brilliant but not vulgar. Titian revealed his many-sided gifts as an artist, capable of reinventing pagan subjects which he called "poesie" with a classical taste that was never rigidly archaeological but richly sensuous. This side of his work led on to Correggio, even though he had no first-hand knowledge of ancient art as yet: it was only in 1545 that Titian finally visited Rome. His visits to Ferrara resulted in a number of portraits, including the delicate *Vincenzo Mosti* in the Pitti Palace (Plate 12).

Alfonso d'Este's cousin, Federico II Gonzaga, *marchese* of Mantua, also sought Titian's presence, tempting him with wealth and also curious gifts: the early works painted in Mantua included the *Portrait of Federico II Gonzaga* (Plate 14, now in the Prado), the *Man with a Glove* (Plate 13) and *Christ Carried to the Tomb* in the Louvre (Plate 11), the first version of a subject he frequently repeated. In this same period, around 1520, Titian received other interesting commissions from different regions of Italy. Outstanding are the imposing *Gozzi Altarpiece* for Ancona and the *Averoldi Polyptych* for the church of the Santi Nazaro and Celso in Brescia (Plates 9, 10). In this case, though Titian had to fit his works into the antiquated form of the polyptych, he conducted extraordinary experiments with light, destined to have a far-reaching influence on the embryonic Brescian school of painting. In 1523 Andrea Gritti was elected Doge, with ambitious plans for innovations in the architecture and art of Venice. Titian was obviously deeply involved in these schemes, and without relinquishing his close contacts with the Este and Gonzaga families once more devoted most of his energies to working in Venice. He painted a fresco of *Saint Cristopher* on the staircase of the Doge's suite in the Palazzo Ducale. This imposing figure reveals his knowledge of the great, exuberant work of il Pordenone, who painted the frescoes decorating the Cappella Malchiostro in the cathedral of Treviso, where Titian painted an *Annunciation* in 1520.

In around 1525 Titian painted the *Altarpiece of the Madonna of Pesaro* for a side altar in the church of the Frari in Venice (Plates 15, 16). This was a work of immense courage, because for the first time Titian abandoned the usual pyramidal structure of the typical "Sacra Conversazione," placing all the figures within a dense network of relationships made up of gestures and glances. The colous are brilliant. Another innovation lies in the tall columns dominating the scene, which instead of defining an architectural setting contained within the limits of the painting, evoke immeasurably vaster spaces. In 1527 Charles V's army sacked Rome and many artist fled from the city, which was put to the sword. Pietro Aretino and the architect and sculptor Jacopo Sansovino left Rome for Venice, and there they soon became part of the city's cultural and artistic life. Titian formed a firm and lasting friedship with both, and while Sansovino prepared to transform the face of Venice with his knowledge of classical architecture and urban design, Pietro Aretino developed a highly effective network of international contacts with the ambassadors of the various courts represented in Venice or even with the rulers themselves. Through him, Titian could count on a series of important contacts and his career received a further boost. In 1528 Titian won the competition for a painting of the *Death of Saint Peter Martyr* for the church of San Zanipolo in Venice, and soon after he made contact with Michelangelo and the Emperor Charles V, whom he met at his coronation in Bologna. Through the support received from Aretino, Titian became the favourite painter of the sovereign "on whose empire the sun never set." Charles V commissioned various portraits (the first shows him with a big dog, and is in the Prado). In 1533 the emperor loaded "el pintor primero" with important honours. For almost forty years Titian enjoyed a privileged relationship with the Spanish court and sent numerous works to Madrid. Meanwhile the Della Rovere family, the lords of Urbino, also patronised Titian. His output never flagged, and now in his forties he organised his workshop with an almost "industrial" degree of efficiency. He did not create a true school, in fat he preferred his collaborators to be reliable and modest, without highly individual styles that could be distinguished from their master's. In this way the atelier opened in Biri Grande sent out a stream of extraordinary originals but also numerous replicas of compositions that had won immediate fame. This was the case with the *Mary Magdalene* executed for the Gonzagas, of which several versions are known (the original is in the Pitti Palace).

Titian produced relatively few works for his own city, so arousing the protests of the Senate, which threatened to suspend payment of the stipend which he received as painter to the state. To quash these complaints and also overcome the competiton of Pordenone, Titian painted works that at once became immensely popular, such as the *Presentation of the Virgin in the Temple* in the Gallerie dell'Accademia (Plate 17) and the *Annunciation* in the Scuola di San Rocco. In Mantua, where Giulio Romano was then active, Titian was commissioned to deliver a group of twelve Roman emperors, the so-called *Twelve "Caesars,"* now lost but widely copied, and a curious portrait of *Isabella d'Este*, now in Vienna, painted from a portrait of *marchesa* from many years earlier. The Della Rovere family also received paintings of great importance, which were nearly all transferred to the Uffizi in the seventeenth-century. Outstanding among them are the portrait of *Duke Guidobaldo della Rovere*, and *Duchess Paola Gonzaga*, but above all the *Venus of Urbino*, completed in 1538 (Plate 18). Thirty years after Giorgione's Dresden Venus, Titian created a new interpretation of this motif: no longer a nude reclining in nature with a dreamy expression, but an immediate, vivid image, a figure that turns a potently seductive gaze on the viewer. The servants busy in the background and the lapdog sleeping on the bed itself give the painting a sense of reality that divests the Venus of any trace of idealization. The same model also posed for another famous painting, now in the Pitti Palace and known as *La Bella*, the embodiment of womanly beauty.

Experiments, Doubts, and Achievements of Late Maturity (1538–1560)

While Titian was being celebrated as a painter of nature, capable of bringing his figures to life, various representatives of the Mannerist school arrived in Venice. This style was then flourishing all over central Italy. The Mannerists sought not to imitate natural effects but to produce an "artificial" or "artful" object, interpreted through a refined intellectual scheme, a subtle code for a small circle of initiates, based on the imitation of the antique and the work of Raphael and Michelangelo. Titian, who had not yet been to Rome, sought to reconcile his own love of colour with the painstaking draughtsmanship of the Mannerists. Certain works from this period reveal unusual concern for the poses of his figures, which are shown in eloquent, rhetorical positions, as in the *Saint John the Baptist* now in the Gallerie dell'Accademia. The *Allocution of Marquis Alfonso d'Avalos* (Plate 19) in the Prado is an excellent example of a harmonious balance between richness of colouring and a classical pose.

These were years of intense activity, during which Titian began to question his own technique. The climax of this conflict created by Mannerism came in around 1541, when he painted the three *Biblical Scenes* for the ceiling of the church of the Santo Spirito in Isola (now in Santa Maria della Salute). These paintings are characterized by dark, heavy outlines and emphatic foreshortening of the scenes. *Christ Crowned with Thorns* (Plate 20), painted between 1542 and 1544 for the church of Santa Maria delle Grazie in Milan and now in the Louvre is the key work in this period. The torturers of Christ are burly, muscular men, reminiscent of Michelangelo's figures; but the sense of tragedy and brutality is expressed through the colouring and the use of light, which gives the image a sense of immediacy and realism.

Titian's experiments with Mannerism appear above all in large-scale religious paintings, while in his portraiture he retains his characteristic frankness and energy. It was in fact in this field that he experimented with a way of handling colour that gradually developed into his new style. Titian no longer took care to unite the brush-strokes into compact areas of colour, but increasingly left the edges ragged and deliberately merely sketched in details with the brush, leaving thick blotches of paint on the canvas. A good example of this technique is the *Portrait of Pietro Aretino* (Florence, Galleria Palatina; Plate 21), described by the subject himself as "a rough sketch rather than a finished work." His portraiture brought the painter into contact with the Farnese family; his portraits of the young *Ranuccio Farnese* (Washington, National Gallery of Art), and *Cardinal Alessandro Farnese* (Naples, Gallerie di Capodimonte) led to Titian's long stay at the Vatican, the guest of Pope Paul III Farnese in 1545–1546.

Finally able to see the masterpieces of classical antiquity (which he described in a letter to Charles V as "marvelous relics") and the works of the Roman Renaissance, Titian was at last able to compare his own style with that of Michelangelo, stimulating debates among the intellectuals on the subject. The Farnese *Danaë* and the *Portrait of Pope Paul III Farnese with his Nephews* (both works now in the Museo di Capodimonte, in Naples; Plates 22, 25) are the most important works from his Roman period. Returning to Venice, Titian painted the *Votive Portrait of the Vendramin Family* (London, National Gallery; Plates 23, 24), and soon after was summoned by Charles V to be present at the Diet of Augsburg. In the German city the Catholic emperor sought a difficult agreement with the Protestant princes, defeated at the battle of Mühlberg. Titian took part in the sessions in 1548 and again in 1551. These occasions produced a series of remarkable portraits (such as that of the emperor on horseback, and another in which he is shown seated, dressed severely in black), as well as "poesie" (such as the first version of *Venus and the Organ Player*, the *Venus and Adonis*, Plate 27, a new version of the *Danaë*) and religious works (*Adoration of the Holy Trinity*), intended for the Spanish court and for the most part hung in the Prado. In 1556, worn out by years of warfare, Charles V abdicated in favour of his son Philip II, who shared his father's love of Titian's art. Philip commissioned further "poesie," a number of portraits and above all paintings of sacred subjects, often somewhat lugubrious in their themes, intended for the Escorial, such as the *Crucifixion*, the *Deposition*, the *Last Supper*, and the *Adoration of the Kings*. Some of the outstanding works of the 1550s may seem to suggest that a certain serenity had been achieved by the master.
A typical work is the luminous, smiling *Venus with Mirror* in the National Gallery of Art, Washington (Plate 28), widely imitated by Rubens and many other artists down to the end of the nineteenth century.
But for many years Titian had been working on a highly demandig painting, the *Martyrdom of Saint Lawrence* (Venice, Gesuiti; Plates 29, 30), exhibited in 1559. All trace of the Renaissance rules of composition have been swept away in the profound darkness of this disturbing nocturne, pierced by fierce points of light (the fire under the gridiron on which the saint is being tortured, the flaming torches, a mystic blaze descending from the heavens, the shining windows in the background). The figures appear amid the glare of the flames, merely sketched in with thick brush-strokes, charged with intense expressive force.
The *Martyrdom of Saint Lawrence*, followed closely by other works using the same techniques, dramatically announced the last period of Titian's art.

A Terrible and Sublime Old Age (1560–1576)

In the course of the 1560s Titian split his output into two main groups: he entrusted his workshop with replicas of original works that had become celebrated and were continually sought after by art merchants and collectors; and he continued to work on new themes himself, producing works which were not always intended for sale. The aged master returned with increasing frequency to Cadore, allowing himself periods of rest and looking after his commercial interests. To

Madonna del Coniglio, 1530; Saint Catherine is a portrait of Titian's wife, who portrayed himself in the guise of the shepherd on the right. Paris, Musée du Louvre.

make himself appear a legendary figure (and also as an excuse for soliciting payments of deferring deadlines for the delivery of new paintings) Titian was in the habit of exaggerating his age. Now well into his seventies, the master was endowed with a physical vigour and creative powers that were truly outstanding. He himself felt proud of these qualities, and signed his great and violent *Annunciation* for the church of San Salvador (1566) "Titianus Fecit Fecit" to stress his unimpaired energy in old age. In his late works, Titian created an even denser, thicker, richer handling: the colours, tending towards darker tones, are treated almost like clay, and no longer have the luminous transparency so characteristic of his early work. Though they include delightfully idyllic paintings (like *Venus Blindfolding Cupid*, Plate 32, from 1565, in the Galleria Borghese, Rome, a charming example of this genre), the subjects are frequently charged with anguish and pathos. The sense of drama, the bitter theme of innocence suffering, grow in intensity until the almost unbearable diapason of the last canvases. During the 1570s Titian painted two self-portraits. In the earlier of the two, now in Berlin, he is depicted in a resolute, commanding pose, which recalls the

Allegory of Prudence, self portrait with his son Marco and nephew Cesare. London, National Gallery.

Titian's Tomb, carved by pupils of Canova. Venice, Santa Maria Gloriosa dei Frari.

portrait of Pietro Aretino twenty years earlier. The figure possesses a certain elegance, and wears a heavy gold chain that was the personal gift of Charles V. In the later self-portrait, now in the Prado, the atmosphere is completely different: the artist is shown in profile and dressed with the utmost simplicity. His features are weary and bear the marks of age; his gaze is lost in the distance, his hand is merely sketched in, a blur of colour, but his fist clutches his brushes with unchanged resolution. The later self-portrait dates from 1567, the years of his portrait of the antiquarian and art merchant *Jacopo Strada* (Vienna, Kunsthistorisches Museum), seized in a moment of professional concentration, handling a precious statue. These intermediaries between artists and purchasers continually hovered around Titian, who was the most famous (and expensive) painter of the time. The steady output of copies by his workshop, always under his rigid control, only partially satisfied the growing demand for his paintings. By 1570, now in his eighties, Titian found himself alone: the death of his old friend Sansovino, worries caused by the indolent character of his eldest son Pomponio, who had taken up an ecclesiastical career without any vocation for it, and the political and military troubles of the Venetian Republic, engaged in wars with the Turks, all weighed heavily on the artist's spirit. Moreover, a fire in the Palazzo Ducale in 1571 destroyed numerous works of art, including some of Titian's official paintings; a second fire in 1577 was even more disastrous. In the last six years of his long life Titian was still capable of profoundly renewing his technique, but the starting point was a careful revisitation of his youthful compositions. The dramatic scene of the *Rape of Lucrece* (the best version, with the figures evoked by large strokes of colour is in the Vienna Akademie der bildenden Künste; Plate 34), repeats the motif of the *Miracle of the Jealous Husband* executed in Padua sixty years earlier; the two figures in the *Nymph and Shepherd* (Vienna, Kunsthistorisches Museum) seem to have emerged from a painting by Giorgione, save that they dissolve into an almost liquefied landscape; the *Christ Crowned with Thorns* in Munich (Plate 35)is almost identical to the dramatic work in the Louvre, but the tragic, clotted colour—almost a huge smear of blood—is wholly new.

Titian was now painting without the least trace of drawing, working furiously with numerous, thick layers of paint. At the feet of *Saint Sebastian* in the Hermitage, for example, there is a reddish-brown mass, shapeless and without any descriptive function: an impasto of colour that harmonizes perfectly with the intense colouring of the landscape. The harsh, disturbing painting of *Apollo and Marsyas* at Kromeriz (Plate 36) shows clearly how Titian pressed the brush onto the canvas, making broad, dense impressions, their outlines blurred. The violence of the feelings expressed, the unusual murkiness of the painted surface, the deliberate dissolving of classical reminiscences in a painting charged with moral and autobiographical overtones, all make this late work one of Titian's greatest masterpieces, looking forward to the final development of his art. This is to be found in the great canvas of the *Pietà* (Plate 37), painted for his own tomb, with a few details still left unfinished when he died. It was completed by Palma il Giovane and is now in the Gallerie dell'Accademia in Venice. The weak light falling from above makes the subject even more moving: the figures, all penetrating psychological portraits, seem to be hemmed in by the massive forms of a classical arch. The figure of Christ is reduced to a ghostly, almost unrecognizable shadow, yet of great intensity, supported by the grieving Madonna and the pathetic, kneeling figure of Nicodemus, in whom we sense a last self-portrait. At the bottom right, almost at the edge of the great canvas, Titian has painted a small ex-voto: the painter with his beloved second son Orazio is shown kneeling in the act of prayer to the Madonna. The insertion of this devotional detail may be related to the terrible outbreak of plague in 1576; in July Orazio was taken to the lazar-house, where he died. On 27 August 1576, in total solitude as the plague was at its height, the great artist died. An exceptional ruling was made to save him from the common grave; but the funeral could not be celebrated with all due ceremony. The material goods of the wealthiest artist of the Renaissance were squandered in less than five years by his son Pomponio. As if by an act of destiny Titian's earthly end was squalid, silent, forlorn; but as a seventeenth-century critic wrote, his fame "lives and will live not just for five hundred years but through all the centuries."

The Legacy

Throughout his very long life, Titian was extolled as an exceptional artist, gifted with almost divine talents. Naturally writers on art from the Veneto described him as the insuperable representative of the local school. In the 1540s a debate flared up between the northern critics, who chose Titian as the perfect artist, and the Tuscans, who exalted Michelangelo. This dispute involved the first principles of art: colour or design? Vasari himself closed the debate provisionally with an open, unmistakable eulogy of Titian, whose only defects, he declared, were an excessive love of lucre—especially in his later years—and his neglect of design. From the mid-sixteenth century on, Titian became a dominant model for all painters. However, he never created a school of his own: he had assistants rather than pupils. Titian preferred not to have assistants with a marked personal style, otherwise purchasers of the paintings sold in his name might have guessed at the presence of different hands in the work. His teaching was mainly indirect, above all concerned with technique. Palma il Giovane recalled this with great vividness in a conversation with Boschini in the mid-seventeenth century, for whom he reconstructed his young manhood in the atelier at Biri Grande. Titian's celebrity was such that not only Venetian artists like Tintoretto and Jacopo Bassano but also numerous late Cinquecento artists sought to follow his example. As Venetian painting entered a decline, Titian's technique influenced the work of Annibale Carracci. But Titian's work was so richly various in its different periods that the changing phases of his work were chosen at different times as models, stimulating the great European masters in different ways. Rubens chose the sumptuous richness of his female nudes and the brilliant highlights of his early work; Caravaggio was influenced by the dramatic qualities of the religious paintings in the depiction of martyrs and saints; Van Dyck studied Titian to endow his portraits with greater variety and vividness; Velasquez learned from his colouring and the blurred edges of his figures; Rembrandt reinvented the rich impasto of his colours. During the eighteenth century, with the birth of Neo-Classicism, Titian's later works, gloomy and blurred, were considered inferior to the earlier paintings. The deliberate choice of a troubled aesthetic, with the paint laid on in thick, heavy brushstrokes, was considered a sign of the master's failing eyesight and sureness of hand. For many decades the "true" Titian was held to be the artist of the *Assunta*, *Sacred and Profane Love*, and the Urbino *Venus*. It was in France, with the Impressionists, that Titian's feeling for light and colour was rediscovered, becoming one of the models for avant-garde artists like Manet and Renoir. At the same time, Cavalcaselle wrote the first full critical study of Titian, analysing sources, publishing his letters and many other unpublished records, and so reconstructing the painter's life and artistic development. In the first half of this century there were numerous new studies, notably those by Berenson, Horticq, Gronau, Tietze. As the date of Titian's birth has never been firmly established, the main doubts concern his early period. In the 1930s the painters of the Roman school, including Scipione and Mafai, offered a contemporary reinterpretation of Titian's art. In the fifties and sixties the leading scholars of Titian were Dell'Acqua, Valcanover and Morassi. In 1976 the fourth centennial of his death was marked by a convention with numerous contributions from scholars from all over the world. In the same year many cities held exhibitions as a tribute to the master. In 1990 the Palazzo Ducale in Venice and the National Gallery of Art in Washington housed an important exhibition devoted to Titian.

1

1. The Miracle of the Wounded Woman, *1511, fresco, 327 × 183 cm. Scuola del Santo, Padua. The group of three frescoes of the* Miracles of Saint Anthony *was the first important commission Titian received. He was then little more than twenty and had come to Padua to escape the plague. Compared with Giorgione, Titian from the start showed an interest in dynamic action, with monumental figures and vivid colours.*

2

3

2. Saint Mark Enthroned, *1511, panel, 230 × 149 cm. Santa Maria della Salute, Venice.*
Commissioned when the plague ended, this altarpiece is essentially a votive offering. Saint Mark, the patron of Venice, is surrounded by the physician-saints Cosma and Damian, on the left, and Saint Roch and Saint Sebastian on the right, traditionally invoked during epìdemics. While respecting the traditional pyramidal organisation of a Renaissance "Sacra Conversazione," the painting is shot through with new tensions, like the cloud of darkness obscuring the visage of Saint Mark.

3. Noli Me Tangere, *c. 1512, canvas, 109 × 91 cm. National Gallery, London.*
Titian's early success with the Venetian public mainly led to commissions for paintings for private devotion, with sacred subjects set in great landscapes.
The "tonalism" of Giorgione and Giovanni Bellini was enriched with a greater density of colours, with strident juxtapositions and unusual reflections, as here in the garments of the Magdalene.

4

4. Sacred and Profane Love, *1515, canvas, 118 × 279 cm. Galleria Borghese, Rome.*
Together with religious works, Titian also painted profane and mythical subjects throughout his life, often with symbolical allusions. The subjects are not always clear: in this case, the title was coined only in the eighteenth century and is not entirely accurate. The allegorical significances do not entirely conceal the constant natural vitality found in all of Titian's work. The refined classicism of his early paintings was a wholly personal achievement, for the artist visited Rome for the first time only in 1545.

5

6

5. The Assunta, *1516–1518, panel, 690 × 360 cm. Santa Maria Gloriosa dei Frari, Venice. This immense altarpiece, placed on the high altar of the Franciscan basilica, marks Titian's conquest of supremacy in Venetian art. When it was unveiled, the painting aroused conflicting reactions: popular enthusiasm contrasted with the misgivings of the friars over the rough yet impressive figures of the Apostles, and the amazement of his fellow painters in Venice, who were unprepared to accept the orchestral crescendo of Titian's colouring. Soon, however, the painting became a landmark in Venetian art. Ludovico Dolce, Titian's first biographer, saw in it the "beauty of Raphael, the* terribilità *of Michelangelo," but above all a natural truthfulness of colouring.*

6. Salome, *c. 1516, canvas, 90 × 72 cm. Galleria Doria Pamphili, Rome. This belongs to a genre of composition highly appreciated by collectors: half-length female figures. During the second decade of the sixteenth century, Titian produced numerous variants on this theme. This work is of particular interest as the head of the Baptist is a self-portrait.*

7

7, 8. The Bacchanals
In 1518 Titian was commissioned to decorate the "alabaster chamber," the private study of Alfonso d'Este, the Duke of Ferrara. The series of paintings took a number of years. Titian painted three canvases (two of which are shown here) and made extensive changes to the landscape in an earlier composition by Giovanni Bellini. The cycle expresses a festive joyfulness, with moments of exalted intoxication yet rendered with unfailing delicacy and good taste. Nearly ten years after the death of Giorgione, Titian has now left behind all memory of the quiet and melancholy harmonies of tonalism and presents images of overwhelming energy. The relation with the Estense court was an enduring one, despite the subsequent competition for his talents by the courts of Mantua and Urbino, which were also among Titian's most important patrons.

7. The Andrians, *1518–1519, canvas, 175 × 193 cm. Prado, Madrid.*

8

8. Bacchus and Ariadne,
1522–1523, canvas,
175 × 190 cm.
National Gallery, London

9

9, 10. Averoldi Polyptych (Polyptych of the Resurrection of Christ), *1520–1522, five panels, painted surface, 278 × 252 cm. Church of Santi Nazaro e Celso, Brescia. Commissioned by the pontifical legate Altobello Averoldi, this work marks an important stage in the development of painting in sixteenth-century Brescia. Despite its antiquated division into five panels, Titian succeeded in giving unity to the complex, largely through the dynamic use of light. To the reflections and highlights suggestive of Giorgione (especially in the left-hand panels) are added the highly innovatory effects of back-lighting in the central panel, in which the Resurrection of Christ is iconographically combined with the Ascension.*

10

11

11. Christ Carried to the Tomb, *c. 1525, canvas, 148 × 225 cm. Louvre, Paris.*
*Painted for Alfonso d'Este, it is one of the earliest interpretations of the theme of the "Transport of the Dead Christ," to which Titian was to return on many occasions, including his last painting (Plate 37). In this case the monumental figures stand out against a sky of veiled luminosity that gives off sparkling gleams of light. The structure of the composition is based on a painting by Raphael (*Baglioni Deposition *with which Titian was familiar through prints. Thus it represents one of the earliest encounters between Titian and the artistic culture of Central Italy, a theme which was to produce important developments in the future.*

12

12. Portrait of Vincenzo Mosti, *c. 1520, panel transferred to canvas, 85 × 66 cm. Galleria Palatina (Palazzo Pitti), Florence.*
The sitter was a dignitary at the Estense court and was portrayed by Titian during one of his numerous stays in Ferrara. The transfer of the painted surface from its original support to canvas has not injured the subtle harmony of the tonalities of grey which determine the refined changes of light and colour that play across the surface of the painting.

13

13. Man with a Glove, *c. 1523, canvas, 100 × 89 cm. Louvre, Paris. The identity of the sitter is uncertain. The painting comes from the collections of the Gonzaga family in Mantua. While exploring the psychology of the man portrayed, Titian also catches his vitality and the sensitivity of his appearance, evident in the gesture and gaze, not rigidly fixed in a static pose.*

14

14. Portrait of Federico II Gonzaga, *c. 1525, canvas, 125 × 99 cm. Prado, Madrid. The* marchese *was the son of Isabella d'Este and patron of Giulio Romano; he was one of the greatest art collectors of the Renaissance. His predilection for Titian is testified by dozens of paintings, of which unhappily not one remains in Mantua. The chronicles of the period tell that Federico Gonzaga sought to win over the painter by sending him precious embroidered robes, perhaps not unlike the spectacular garment worn in this portrait, painted by Titian with great virtuosity.*

15, 16. Altarpiece of the Madonna of Pesaro, *1522–1526, 278 × 268 cm. Santa Maria Gloriosa dei Frari, Venice. Commissioned in 1519 by Bishop Jacopo Pesaro to celebrate a naval victory and also as a collective tribute to the Virgin by the Pesaro family, this great altarpiece took a very long time to complete. Titian here makes a break with the Renaissance scheme of the Madonna enthroned. As the painting was intended for a side altar, Titian has moved the Madonna to the right, with a new organisation of the composition, which brings together all the figures through a tightly-knit concatenation of gestures and glances.*

15

18

18. Venus of Urbino, *1538, canvas, 119 × 165 cm. Uffizi, Florence.*
Commissioned by Guidobaldo della Rovere, Lord of Urbino, this work marks a decisive step forward compared with earlier images of Venus reclining. Comparison with the Dresden Venus, *painted by Giorgione and Titian in collaboration around 1510, reveals the transition from serene contemplation of female beauty to intense sensuousness: Venus is not sleeping amid the quiet of nature, but reclines on a bed and gazes seductively at the viewer. The lap dog curled up on the bed and the servants in the background give the painting an immediacy that makes the presence of the delightful nude all the more vivid and alluring.*

19

19. The Allocution of Marquis Alfonso d'Avalos, *1540–1541, 223 × 165 cm. Prado, Madrid. The noble and declamatory gesture of the marquis of Vasto and Pescara, the governor of Milan, descends directly from the classical repertoire. Alfonso d'Avalos is shown in the pose of* adlocutio *(address) typical of a Roman consul or emperor. This direct reference to ancient sculpture marks Titian's closest approach to Central Italian Mannerism, which he encountered in the work of important Tuscan masters, such as Francesco Salviati and Giorgio Vasari, who were in Venice in the years around 1540.*

20. Christ Crowned with Thorns, *1542–1544, panel, 303 × 180 cm. Louvre, Paris. Painted for the church of Santa Maria delle Grazie in Milan, this is an example of Titian's highly personal interpretation of Mannerism. The poses and the anatomy of the figures are clearly related to Michelangelo's* terribilità *and to classical statuary. The dramatic handling of light and the tragic force of the gestures are, however, revisions of the rigid stylistic code of the Mannerists and move in the direction of a harsh, troubled naturalism.*

20

21

21. Portrait of Pietro Aretino, *1545, canvas, 98 × 78 cm. Galleria Palatina, Florence.*
This was a "private" portrait painted shortly before Titian's visit to Rome. It is evidence of the close friendship and firm professional ties between Titian and the Tuscan writer. The portrait was so new in technique that Aretino judged it to be "rather a sketch than a finished work." Titian was experimenting with the technique that was to become typical of his last period: the outlines are no longer clearly defined, and the broad brush-strokes seem to have been made rapidly, as if to sketch in the sitter rather than describe him. The result is a vital animation certainly deliberately opposed to the cold stylistic elegance of contemporary Central Italian portraitists.

22

22. Danaë, *1545, canvas, 117 × 96 cm. Gallerie di Capodimonte, Naples. Begun in Venice and completed in Rome, this painting was Titian's personal gift to the refined Cardinal Alessandro Farnese (the nephew of Pope Paul III) who had brought him to Rome. While it was still no more than a sketch,* monsignor *Della Casa described it to Cardinal Farnese as "A nude that will put the devil into you." Titian gave the image of Danaë, visited by Zeus in the form of shower of gold, a vibrant sensuousness, even more vitally alive than the* Venus of Urbino *(Plate 18). To quote* monsignor *Della Casa again compared with the Farnese Danaë, the* Venus of Urbino *"looked like a nun."*

23

23, 24. Votive Portrait of the Vendramin Family, *1543–1547, canvas, 206 × 310 cm. National Gallery, London. Three generations of the important patrician family are shown adoring a reliquary of the True Cross. This great group portrait is an excellent example of Titian's entrepreneurial flair: the painting was begun before his journey to Rome, left deliberately unfinished in the workshop, and completed only when he returned to Venice. In this way he created a sense of expectation for his return, with an only temporary absence from Venetian art circles.*

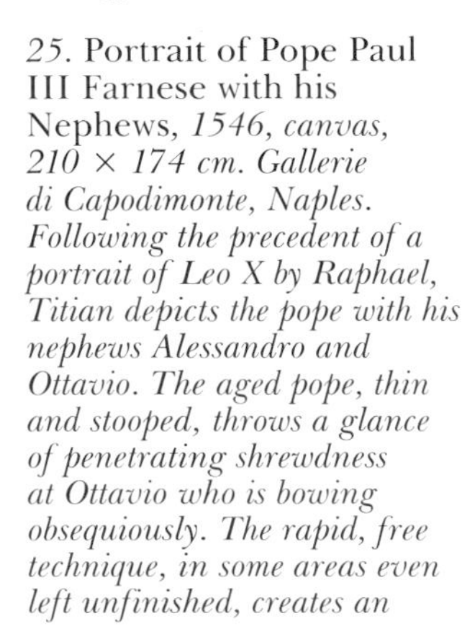

25

25. Portrait of Pope Paul III Farnese with his Nephews, *1546, canvas, 210 × 174 cm. Gallerie di Capodimonte, Naples. Following the precedent of a portrait of Leo X by Raphael, Titian depicts the pope with his nephews Alessandro and Ottavio. The aged pope, thin and stooped, throws a glance of penetrating shrewdness at Ottavio who is bowing obsequiously. The rapid, free technique, in some areas even left unfinished, creates an impression of intrigue and oppressiveness. The colouring is thick and even richer than before, with red predominating. One of Titian's maxims was that a painter needs to knows only three colours, white, red and black, "and be able to use them."*

26. Portrait of Charles V on Horseback, *1548, canvas, 322 × 279 cm. Prado, Madrid. This great canvas was completed by Titian during his first journey to the city of Augsburg, the scene of the meeting between Charl... and the German prin... had embraced Luther... The triumphal image... sovereign... important... against... at Muh... example... portrait... widely... courtly... Velasq... centur...*

26

27

27. Venus and Adonis, *1553, canvas, 186 × 207 cm. Prado, Madrid.*
Painted for Philip II of Spain, the successor to Charles V, this work interprets the mythological subject with great refinement of detail but at the same times has intensely melancholy overtones. Titian explained the pose of the Venus in a letter to Philip II: since he had already painted a Venus for him, shown reclining and seen from the front, he had decided to send him a view of her from behind, to be set opposite the other one in his private chamber, and so "make a fine scene."

28

28. Venus with Mirror, *1555, canvas, 124 × 105 cm. National Gallery of Art, Washington. This is the principal version of a highly successful subject, of which numerous replicas were painted by his workshop, while it was frequently imitated by Baroque artists, notably Rubens. It is interesting to note that this painting was never sold by Titian but remained in his workshop and was sold to the Barberigo family in 1581, five years after his death.*

29, 30. Martyrdom of Saint Lawrence, *1548–1559, transferred canvas, 500 × 280 cm. Church of the Gesuiti, Venice. The extremely long time spent on this painting was due to the astonishing number of innovations made by Titian in it. It was executed for the funerary chapel of a nobleman, Lorenzo Massolo, in the church of the Crociferi, later taken over by the Jesuits. Titian here abandoned all trace of Renaissance tradition, in a violently expressionistic work based on dramatic use of light. The deep darkness is lit up by violent glares within the scene, so creating a profoundly impressive effect. The theatrical foreshortening of the receding architectural backdrop, the animation of the figures, the thick, rapid brush-strokes, all make this painting a forerunner of Titian's last phase.*

29

31

31. Diana and Actaeon, *1558, canvas, 190 × 207 cm. National Gallery of Scotland, Edinburgh. This is one of a cycle of paintings devoted to the myth of Diana and intended for Philip II. In his transition from the works of his late maturity to those of old age, Titian had not lost his love for vivid colours and refined details (the basin in the centre of the painting shows that his virtuosity in reproducing objects was as strong as ever), but here it is enriched by a dense, tremulous, animated handling.*

32

32. Venus Blindfolding Cupid, *1565, canvas, 118 × 185 cm. Galleria Borghese, Rome. This is a classical intermezzo in the midst of the increasingly tragic output of Titian's last years. The colours are all light tones, inspired by the hues of the rosy sunset in the background. The versatility of Titian's brushwork is immensely resourceful and varied: from the minute, compact rendering of certain details to the broad impressions of the spatula used for the garments.*

33

33. Self-Portrait, *1567, canvas, 86 × 65 cm. Prado, Madrid.*
This is the last "independent" image that Titian left of himself; other self portraits are inserted in later canvases but in very animated settings.
Here the artist, by now almost eighty years old, makes no attempt to conceal the signs of his physical aging. Beneath them, however, shines an inexhaustible creative energy, expressed most clearly in the alert gaze and the way that his hand firmly grasps the brush.

34

34. The Rape of Lucrece, *c. 1570, canvas, 140 × 100 cm. Akademie der bildenden Künste, Vienna. This is Titian's "private" version of a subject repeated a number of times around 1570. After sixty years, Titian repeated the theme of the* Miracle of the Jealous Husband *in the fresco in Padua. The relationship between the two figures is equally dynamic, but the meaning of the drama is here even more violent, as appears in the flickering, melting colouring, laid thickly on the canvas.*

35

36

35. Christ Crowned with Thorns, *c. 1570, canvas, 280 × 182 cm. Alte Pinakothek, Munich. In this painting the relationship with the* Christ Crowned with Thorns *(Plate 20) in the Louvre appears clearly from the composition, but here the murky colour, almost dripped onto the canvas, increases the harsh, tormented rendering of the brutality of the drama. A comparison between the two paintings also brings out the disappearance of the classical elements, which in the earlier work were a tribute to Mannerist ideals.*

36. Apollo and Marsyas, *c. 1575, canvas, 212 × 207 cm. National Museum, Komeriz. The painting represents the punishment of the satyr Marsyas, defeated by Apollo in a musical contest and condemned to be flayed alive by the god. The grimy colouring, the violence of the image and the composition inverted towards the viewer all make this one of the strongest paintings of the Cinquecento.*

37

37. Pietà, *1576, canvas, 351 × 389 cm. Galleria dell'Accademia, Venice. This is Titian's last work, painted when he was nearly ninety for his own tomb. The few details left unfinished were completed by Jacopo Palma il Giovane, but partly because of the plague that was raging at the time, it was never placed on Titian's sepulchre. This is the final stage of the dissolution of the image almost into a clotted impasto of light and colour (note Christ's right hand, reduced to a spectral shadow), and it contains anguished autobiographical references: the pathetic figure of Nicodemus, kneeling to support Christ under the armpits, is a bleak self-portrait, while on the far right of the painting, under the statue of the Sybil of the Hellespont, there appears a tiny votive painting, in which Titian and his son Orazio are praying devoutly to the Madonna.*

Where to see Titian

Titian's career spanned an exceptional total of seven decades, during which time he was continually inventing and developing new forms, techniques, and compositions: the catalogue of his surviving works includes over five hundred titles.

Titian almost always painted in oil on canvas, developing special applications of the technique. Exceptions to this are provided by a few juvenile works and altarpieces like the *Assunta* and the *Averoldi Polyptych*, painted on board. His frescoes are rare, as the technique was little used in Venice for obvious reasons of climate.

A number of Titian's works have been lost over the course of time: we still have engravings, copies, drawings, or descriptions of some of these.

The most serious gap is the *Assassination of Saint Peter Martyr*, painted between 1528 and 1530 for San Zanipolo and burned on August 16, 1867. Another fire in 1571 had already destroyed a painting that Titian had done for the Dominicans of San Zanipolo, the *Last Supper* in the refectory, which was replaced by Veronese's *Feast in the House of Levi*. In 1577 the canvases in the Doge's Palace (official portraits of the doges, the *Battle of Cadore*, the votive painting of Andrea Gritti) were burned.

Another painful loss was that of twelve effigies of Roman emperors, swallowed up by the sea when the ship taking them to Spain sank in 1652. In addition to the loss of several of the over sixty pictures intended for the court of Spain, significant works have vanished from Vicenza (*Judgment of Solomon* in the Palazzo del Capitano), Brescia (three canvases on the ceiling of the City Hall), and Novara (*Nativity* in the Cathedral).

Works in Italy

Only a quarter of Titian's output is in Italy. The artist spent almost the whole of his life in Venice, but did much of his work for clients from abroad. Consequently the group of works that remains in Venice is extremely important but not very numerous. Florence and Naples also possess prestigious groups, inherited from the family collections of the Della Rovere (originally in Urbino) and Farnese (once in Rome), while the dispersion of the Este and Gonzaga collections has meant that there are no more works by Titian in Ferrara and Mantua, two cities where the master spent time and left behind dozens of canvases.

Venice

A fair number of paintings can still be seen in the artist's birthplace. We shall start our tour in the basilica of Santa Maria Gloriosa dei Frari, where the master's tomb is also to be found. On the high altar stands the splendid *Assunta* (1516-1518), the most ambitious altarpiece painted by Titian. The *Altarpiece of the Madonna of Pesaro*, finished in 1525, is on an altar on the left-hand side.

The nearby Scuola di San Rocco also houses significant works: the devotional *Christ Carrying the Cross*, which has also been attributed to Giorgione, and an *An-*

nunciation (c. 1540). Not far from San Rocco and the Frari, the Gallerie dell'Accademia incorporates the old seat of the Scuola della Carità, which contains the *Presentation of the Virgin in the Temple* (1538). The museum also displays the noble *Saint John the Baptist* (1542) and above all the moving *Pietà* (1576), the painter's last work.
The sacristy of the nearby basilica of Santa Maria della Salute houses a group of paintings that were formerly in the church of Santo Spirito in Isola: the juvenile altarpiece depicting *Saint Mark Enthroned* (1511), the decoration of the ceiling (1542-1544: three *Scenes from the Bible* and ten *Busts of Saints*), and the *Pentecost*.
Coming to Saint Mark's, it is worth mentioning the possibility that Titian supplied the cartoons for some of the mosaics in the basilica. Only a few of the pictures executed for the seat of government by the official Painter to the Republic are left in the Doge's Palace: the fresco of *Saint Christopher* from 1524 and the *Votive Painting of Doge Grimani*, begun in 1555. A watchful eye is kept on Saint Mark's Library by the *Allegory of Wisdom*, datable to 1559.
Entering the Mercerie, we come to the church of San Salvador, where the *Transfiguration* (1560) stands on the high altar while the *Annunciation* (1566) is set on an altar on the right. A few steps away lies the Fondaco dei Tedeschi: fragments of the frescoes that used to adorn the building are now in the Galleria Franchetti in the Ca' d'Oro, which also has an elegant version of the *Venus with Mirror* (1555). Not far past the Rialto Bridge stands the church of San Giovanni Elemosinario, where Titian painted the altarpiece of the church's patron, *Saint John the Almsgiver* (1545).
Another extraordinary masterpiece is the *Martyrdom of Saint Lawrence* in the church of the Jesuits, whose festive baroque decoration seems curiously out of keeping with the dramatic painting.

Veneto
There are several juvenile works by Titian in Padua: two *Mythological Scenes* in the Museo Civico and above all the three *Miracles of Saint Anthony* (1511) in the Scuola del Santo.
The Malchiostro Chapel in Treviso Cathedral, frescoed by Pordenone, has an *Annunciation* (1520) on the altar, while the Museo Civico contains a *Portrait of Sperone Speroni*. There is a late *Assunta* (1535) in Verona Cathedral.
Works by Titian can be found in the parish churches of a number of minor centres: the *Madonna with Saint Titian* at Pieve di Cadore (Belluno) and the *Sacra Conversazione* at Serravalle (an outlying ward of Vittorio Veneto, Treviso).

Lombardy
Undoubtedly the most important painting by Titian in Lombardy is the *Averoldi Polyptych* (1520-1522) in the Brescian church of Santi Nazaro e Celso.
A number of works of some value can be seen in the museums of Milan: a *Saint Jerome* and the *Portrait of Count Porcia* in Brera; the *Old Man in Armor* and a late *Adoration of the Magi* in the Ambrosiana; the *Portrait of the Ambassador of Aramont* in the Castello Sforzesco.
There are a *Madonna and Child* and an *Orpheus and Eurydice*, dating from Titian's youth, in the Accademia Carrara in Bergamo. The parish church of Medole (Mantua) has an altarpiece representing the *Risen Christ Appearing to his Mother* (c. 1550).

Florence
The Medici collections, split between the Uffizi and Palazzo Pitti, have been enriched by groups of paintings from the Della Rovere court in Urbino, as well as by canvases from every period of the artist's career that have made their way to Florence at different times. They include the *Flora* (1516), the *Urbino Venus* (1538), and the *Portraits of Francesco Maria Della Rovere and Paola Gonzaga* (1536-1538) in the Uffizi; the *Concert*, once attributed to Giorgione, the *Beauty* (1537), and the portraits of *Vincenzo Mosti* (1520) and *Pietro Aretino* (1545) in the Galleria Palatina.

Marche
The only painting of the many that Titian produced for the Ducal Palace in Urbino to have survived is a standard with the *Last Supper* and the *Resurrection*, painted around 1542.
The Pinacoteca Civica of Ancona contains the forceful *Gozzi Altarpiece* (1520), while the church of San Domenico houses a *Crucifixion* from 1558. Finally, there is a *Saint Francis with the Stigmata* in the Museo Civico of Ascoli Piceno.

Rome
The capital's museums are rich in juvenile works by Titian. The *Baptism of Christ* (1512) is in the Pinacoteca Capitolina; the *Salome with the Baptist's Head* (1516) is in the Galleria Doria; the Galleria Borghese houses the celebrated *Sacred and Profane Love* (1514), along with another beautiful painting of a profane subject, *Venus blindfolding Cupid* (1565). The large *Sacra Conversazione* (1538) that was originally on the altar of the church of San Nicolò in Venice is now in the Vatican Art Gallery.

Naples
The Gallerie di Capodimonte have inherited the Farnese Collection, containing many splendid canvases by Titian, including the *Portrait of Pope Paul III Farnese with his Nephews*, the *Danaë*, and the *Portrait of Cardinal Alessandro Farnese*, all dating from the Roman period (1545-1546). The church of San Domenico Maggiore houses an *Annunciation* (c. 1557). It is also worth mentioning the *Saint Francis receiving the Stigmata* in the Museo Pepoli in Trapani.

Works Located Abroad
Many of Titian's paintings were intended for export right from the start. Since then they have been even more widely scattered by the art market. The formation of the most significant collections (in Madrid, Vienna, London, and Paris) marks particular phases in the history of taste and collecting.

Spain
The group of around thirty canvases in the Museo del Prado in Madrid form the largest corpus of Titian's works in the world. Among the best known of these are the two *Bacchanalia* (1518-1520, formerly in Ferrara), the *Exhortation of Alfonso d'Avalos* (1541), the portraits of *Charles V* and *Philip II*, the *Venus with Organ Player* (1550), the *Farewell of Venus to Adonis* (1553), the *Adoration of the Trinity* (1551-1554), and the last *Self Portrait* (1570).
Among other paintings, the Thyssen Bornemisza Collection, recently moved from Lugano to Madrid, contains the *Portrait of Doge Francesco Venier* and a *Madonna and Child*.
In the monastery of the Escorial are housed various works sent by Titian to Spain toward the end of his life: the *Saint Margaret*, a *Crucifix*, a specially produced version of the *Martyrdom of Saint Lawrence*, and the *Last Supper*.

Vienna
The set of pictures in Vienna's Kunsthistorisches Museum is not much smaller and is made up of works that are perhaps even more evenly distributed over the entire span of Titian's career.
The initial nucleus comes from the Habsburg collections: it ranges from delightful early works, like the *Madonna delle Ciliegie* and *Violante*, through paintings from his maturity, such as the *Portrait of Isabella d'Este* and *Christ and the Woman Taken in Adultery*, and extends all the way up to two canvases from the final period, *Nymph and Shepherd* and *Portrait of the Antiquarian Jacopo Strada*. There is also a vigorous *Portrait of a Gentleman in Armor* in the Residenzgalerie in Salzburg.

London
The paintings in the National Gallery of London have been acquired from a variety of British private collections, as well as through an aggressive policy of purchases over the last few centuries.
The sequence includes mythological subjects (*Bacchus and Ariadne*, *Diana and Actaeon*), the *Noli me tangere*, still heavily influenced by Giorgione, and a number of fine portraits, among them the so-called Ariosto, the *Schiavona*, and *The Vendramin Family*.
The National Gallery in Edinburgh houses important mythological canvases, such as the juvenile *Three Ages of Man* and the two episodes from the myth of Diana (c. 1558). There are other works in British private collections, including the *Perseus and Andromeda* in the Wallace Collection in London and the *Flight into Egypt* in that of the Marquis of Bath.

Paris
The series in the Louvre opens with a question mark: whether the *Country Concert* should be attributed to Titian or Giorgione. The other paintings are chiefly from the artist's juvenile period or early maturity, like the *Christ Carried to the Tomb* (1525), formerly in the Este collections, or the large *Christ Crowned with Thorns* (1542-1544), originally in Milan. Interesting iconographic questions are raised by the *Venus of the Leopard*

and *the Allegory of Alfonso d'Avalos*, while the *Madonna del Coniglio* (1530) has biographical implications.

Germany
The Alte Pinakothek in Munich possesses two masterpieces, the *Portrait of Charles V Seated* (1548) and the *Christ Crowned with Thorns*, one of the artist's last paintings.
In the collections of the Staatliche Museen in Berlin there are several portraits, including the *Self Portrait* of 1562, and an excellent version of the *Venus with Organ Player* (circa 1550). The Gemäldegalerie in Dresden boasts the celebrated *Dresden Venus*, painted by Giorgione and finished by Titian, and works from the Este Collection, such as the *Christ of the Coin* and a *Portrait of a Young Woman in White*, sometimes identified as Titian's daughter Lavinia.

Other Locations in Europe
Two very great masterpieces from the last phase of the painter's career are in the Residence of Kromeriz (in the Czech Republic) and the Hermitage in Saint Petersburg: the *Apollo and Marsyas* and *Saint Sebastian* respectively. The Royal Museums in Antwerp contain the important early altarpiece depicting *Jacopo Pesaro in front of Saint Peter*, while the Boymans-van Beunigen Museum in Rotterdam possesses the *Child with Two Dogs*. There are two fine portraits in Copenhagen's Statens Museum.

United States
A large number of canvases of great beauty can be seen in American museums. Outstanding examples in the Frick Collection in New York are a *Portrait of a Youth in a Red Hat* (c. 1515) and a version of the *Portrait of Pietro Aretino*.
There is a larger group in the National Gallery of Washington, including several extraordinary works like Giovanni Bellini's *Feast of the Gods*, completed by Titian and hung in the study of Alfonso d'Este, the *Portrait of Pietro Bembo* (c. 1540), the *Vision of Saint John the Evangelist*, formerly set on the ceiling of the Scuola Grande di San Giovanni Evangelista in Venice, and the fascinating *Venus with Mirror* (1555). Finally, the Isabella Stewart Gardner Museum in Boston houses one of the artist's finest mythological works, the *Rape of Europe*.

Anthology of Comments

I have completed the painting of the Magdalene which your Excellency ordered from me, with the greatest dispatch possible, in less than a month, leaving aside all other work I had on hand. In it I have sought to express what one expects of this art; and if I have been successful I leave the judgement to others. If my pen had matched the great thoughts I had in my soul, I believe I should have satisfied the desire I have to serve your excellency, but I fell far short.
(Titian, *Letter to the Marquis of Mantua*, 14 April 1531)

He walks with equal step with nature: so that his every figure lives, moves, and the flesh trembles... In this painting [the *Assunta*] there is the greatness and overwhelming power of Michelangelo, the beauty and delightfulness of Raphael, and the colouring of nature herself. Clumsy painters and the foolish rabble, who had before this seen nothing but the dead, cold works of the Bellinis and Vivarini, without life and movement, spoke a great deal of ill of this painting. But when envy had cooled, people began to marvel at the new style Titian had created in Venice. And truly it can be called a miracle that Titian, without having seen the antiquities of Rome at that time, painted this only with the weak glimmering of light he had discovered in Giorgione.
(L. Dolce, *L'Aretino. Dialogo della pittura*, 1557)

Titian was healthy and strong, more than anyone else has ever been; and he never received anything save favours and happiness from heaven. To his home in Venice there came all the princes, men of letters, and gentlemen that ever were in Venice during his lifetime; for besides his excellence in art he was of gentle manners, courteous and sweet-natured. He had some rivals in Venice, but none of great value, so that he surpassed them easily through the excellence of his art, and he was skilled at entertaining gentlemen and making himself agreeable to them. He earned a great deal of money, for his works always fetched good sums...
When Vasari, the writer of this account, was in Venice in 1566, he went to visit Titian, as they were good friends, and found him, old as he was, still with his brushes in his hand, and he had great pleasure in seeing his works and conversing with him.
(G. Vasari, *Vite de' più eccellenti pittori, scultori et architettori*, ed. 1568)

Titian was truly the most excellent of all painters; for his brush always gave birth to expressions of life. Giacomo Palma il Giovane... told me that he laid out his paintings as a great mass of colours, which served (so to speak) as a bed, on which he based his images as he intended to create them: and I too have seen him make decisive brushstrokes thick with paint; sometimes a streak of *terra rossa*, which (he said) he used for half-tones, and at others a brush laden with white-lead and reds and black and yellow with which he formed a highlight, and

so with four brush-strokes he created the promise of a rare figure. After having formed these precious foundations, he turned his paintings to the wall and left them for some months without looking at them: and when he wanted to work on them again, he would examine them rigorously as if they had been his deadly enemies, to see if there were any defects in them, and finding some things that did not agree with his delicate understanding, like a beneficent surgeon he would remedy the ailment... Working in this way, and re-shaping those figures, he transformed them into the most perfect symmetry, representing beauty in nature and art; and after having done this, he would turn his hand to other things until they were dry and repeat the process; and from time to time he would then clothe those quintessences with flesh, repainting them many times, until all they lacked was the living breath. Nor did he ever paint a figure at the first attempt; for he used to say that he that improvises cannot form a learned verse or one that is well-made. But the modifications of his last re-touchings consisted in rubbing in the highlights with his fingers, blending in the half-tones and uniting one tone with another. At other times he would use his fingers to place a dab of dark colour in some corner to strengthen it, or some streak of red to enliven some superficial feeling, and so he would go on perfecting his animated figures. And Palma assured me that in finishing his paintings he painted with his fingers more than his brushes.
(M. Boschini, *Le ricche miniere della pittura veneziana*, 1674)

It is time now to go on to Tiziano Vecellio, as the reader perhaps desires. I cannot satisfy him as I would like to, for where the work of an artist is great, everything that one can write is surpassed by his merit, and in a way demeans him. But since a precise indication of what distinguishes an artist among all others is worth much more than a vague commendation, I shall quote the judgement of an excellent critic, who used to say that Titian saw nature and painted it truly better than anyone else; to which I shall add that he was among the painters with the deepest understanding of nature, and a universal master; for whether he painted figures, or landscapes, or any other subject, he expressed its true nature in his paintings. From birth he possessed a firm, serene, wise spirit, inclined towards the truth rather than the new and the specious; and it is this spirit that forms both true writers and true painters.
(L. Lanzi, *Storia pittorica dell'Italia*, 1795–1796)

But Titian had reached not only a very great age but also a perfect knowledge of the secrets of nature... His power was the outcome of long years of experience that made each brush-stroke confident and expressive. But at the same time the years had made him completely realistic and practice had given him the ability to depict the truth with great mastery in its main features but not always with fidelity in the rendering of particulars, as appears in the more studied and perhaps more timid style of the early period of his splendid career. But it would be an error to think that the seeming facility of the works from his last period were the result of mere rapidity of conception and execution. Instead we feel that Titian devoted more time and study to these than one might think, and that especially in these paintings there is one of his greatest gifts, the ability to conceal that effort that he always made under the appearance of the greatest naturalness and spontaneousness of execution.
(G.B. Cavalcaselle, A. Crowe, *Tiziano: la sua vita e i suoi tempi*, 1878)

In all of the youthful Titian there is something Phidian; even his impasto has the living quality of Greek marble: it has the same sublimated, innocent sensuousness, when compared with the overcharged rank sensuousness of the later Giorgione. I said the bodies were sketched in roughly; and it is precisely at the borders of every chromatic area that Titian leaves the freedom of a shifting sketch, a changing, growing life. Delicately wrinkled, burnt, liquefied colour, swarming touches of paint suggestive of Cézanne's "scars" when he sought to render reality; all this Titian did effortlessly. This was happening in Venice while Raphael was painting the Stanze in the Vatican, and

Michelangelo, craning his neck and cursing, was completing the vault of the Sistine Chapel.
(R. Longhi, *Viatico per cinque secoli di pittura veneziana*, 1946)

The premonitions of a transcendental world become more powerful in his last period, when Titian continued a process of synthesis of the most audacious experiments that painting has ever attempted. It was a conception that corresponded to a new way of understanding painting, not as a merely artistic rendering of visible nature but as a search for a symbol, for the last essence embodied in things as the ultimate, profound truth. Light suffuses forms like a flame, melting them, dissolving them, blurring their outlines, so that everything seems to be traversed by a fluctuating vibrancy. Titian's world was on the very threshold of the modern world, which it divined and heralded.
(A. Morassi, *Tiziano*, 1964)

[In his portraits] what distinguishes his style, especially in comparison with that of his imitators, are those broad strokes of colour that always seize the figure in a moment, outside the temporal continuity which is our normal experience, and brings out its whole being, to the point where movement is stilled, overwhelmed by the thickening of the zones of colour, and it becomes possible to enjoy the spectacle of a lining stitched to the outside of a garment, a throat and shoulders emerging from between the bands of a fur collar. But it is clear that this is a moment of stasis in movement; for the recomposition of these planes, even in figures posing for a portrait, is always accomplished, generating the space of the painting.
(A. Ballarin, *Tiziano*, 1968)

This is the memory which later generations have of Titian: the image of a happy man, whose ambitions, both of an artistic and social nature, had been satisfied. But we often forget something which was quite obvious to his contemporaries, that is to say, that he would never touch a paintbrush except on commission. Works which were the expression of indisputably sincere emotions and incomparable technical skill were for him, when they were ready to leave his studio, just so many objects with which to trade, barter and corrupt.
(R. and M. Wittkower, *Born under Saturn*, 1968)

Portraiture occupied Titian throughout his long life. His development from an initial lyrical hedonism to a conscious fullness of life and human values, and then the final blaze which devoured reality and matter to lay bare the essence, was a wholly inward development. Having destroyed in his early work the pictorial isolation of man from the world around him, through an artistic conception that fused the two in a vibrant atmosphere of movement, Titian "made the human figure the yardstick and centre of his art," deepening its truth, character, dignity, a symbol justifying its existence through the years. His progress was solitary, for no important influence appears in his portraits.
(M. Garberi, "Tiziano: i ritratti," in *Omaggio a Tiziano*, exhibition catalogue, Palazzo Reale, Milan 1976)

The combination of richness and intensity of hue which Titian achieves in the individual colours is made possible by his use of the oil medium, but his desire to present these primary hues at such a level of saturated intensity and his way of putting them together is an aesthetic choice. Thus Titian limits his colours in order to bring them into a new kind of accord. "The colourisation of which Titian was the originator," Theodore Hetzer wrote in German in 1935, "is characterised by the fact that his fidelity to nature is bound up with an arrangement of colours which in its independent character displays the internal order of the world and its associations, relationships and connections." We may not wish to express ourselves so metaphysically, but in practice our experience of the essential rightness of Titian's colour harmonies confirms what Hetzer says, and shows that Titian achieves through colour a harmonious but active balance of opposing forces in a manner strictly comparable to what Raphael achieved through form.
(J. Steer, "Titian and Venetian Colour," in *The Genius of Venice 1500–1600*, exhibition catalogue, Royal Cademy of Arts, London 1983)

But Titian was already preparing a new surprise.
In May 1518 he placed on the high altar of the church of the Frari a large painting commissioned two years earlier, the *Assumption of the Virgin*.
The increasing scale of the figures, which are of heroic dimensions, the accentuated tension of movement, a greater freedom in the composition, so that all the attitudes of the figures seem less studied and more natural, and even an intense, contrasting colouring confer a highly dramatic narrative tone on the painting, which clashed with the wishes of the church that had commissioned it. Many people clearly found it hard to accept this "restless" phase of Titian's work.
(M. Lucco, "La pittura a Venezia nel primo Cinquecento", in *La Pittura in Italia. Il Cinquecento*, 1988)

It is extremely vague to talk of "Titian's technique," if not inaccurate. Over seventy years of activity, the artist varied his method of painting profoundly, from the luminous, tonal manner of his early period to the heavy, murky brush-strokes of the last, overwhelming canvases. The unifying element in his style, from his early work to the last paintings, is the sense of colour as the material that "makes" a painting. Perhaps no other artist has ever had such an acute, physical, tactile feeling for paint clotted densely on the palette and tranferred to the image on the canvas.
(F. Caroli, S. Zuffi, *Tiziano*, 1990)

Titian's definitive break with naturalistic illusionism, which was beginning to suffer from academic involution coincided with the arrival in Venice of the Tuscan artists Francesco Salviati and Giuseppe Porta in 1539, and of Giorgio Vasari in 1541.
Titian was well aware of the shift toward Mannerism in the Venetian school of painting of which he was once again undisputed leader following Pordenone's death in 1539. Lorenzo Lotto's presence was in creasingly sporadic, Girolamo Savoldo's poetic nocturnes more and more isolated...
Titian's sympathy for the "maniera" was not, however, substantial—it did not include the spiritual world of mannerism but served merely to give greater expressive licence and immediacy in terms of lighting technique, while colour would always have the last word.
The maturing of this moment in his career was exceptionally quick.
(F. Valcanover, "Introduction to Titian", exhibition catalogue, Palazzo Ducale, Venice 1990)

Essential Bibliography

A. Morassi, *Tiziano*, Milan 1964.

A. Ballarin, *Tiziano*, Florence 1968.

E. Panofsky, *Problems on Titian, mostly Iconographic*, New York 1969.

F. Valcanover, *L'opera completa di Tiziano*, Milan 1969.

R. Pallucchini, *Tiziano*, Florence 1969.

H.E. Wethey, *The paintings of Titian*, London 1969–1980.

Omaggio a Tiziano. La cultura milanese nell'età di Carlo V, exhibition catalogue, Palazzo Reale, Milan 1976.

Tiziano e il Manierismo europeo, Florence 1978.

S.J. Freedberg, *The Pelican History of Art. Painting in Italy 1500–1600*, Harmondsworth, Middlesex 1979.

C. Hope, *Titian*, London 1980.

Tiziano e Venezia, papers from the international study conference (Venice 1976), Vicenza 1980.

Da Tiziano a El Greco. Per la storia del manierismo a Venezia, exhibition catalogue, Palazzo Ducale, Venice 1981.

D. Rosand, *Tiziano*, Milan 1983.

The Genius of Venice, 1500-1600, exhibition catalogue, Royal Academy of Arts, London 1983.

F. Caroli, S. Zuffi, *Tiziano*, Milan 1990.

Titian, exhibition catalogue, Palazzo Ducale, Venice 1990.